GEORGE W.
BUSH

PRESIDENTIAL ✦ LEADERS

GEORGE W. BUSH

HERÓN MÁRQUEZ

TWENTY-FIRST CENTURY BOOKS / MINNEAPOLIS

Twenty-First Century Books
A division of Lerner Publishing Group
241 First Avenue North
Minneapolis, MN 55401 U.S.A.

Website address: www.lernerbooks.com

Library of Congress Cataloging-in-Publication Data

Herón Márquez
    George W. Bush / by Herón Márquez
        p. cm. — (Presidential leaders)
    Includes bibliographical references and index.
    ISBN-13: 978–0–8225–1507–4 (lib.bdg.: alk paper)
    ISBN-10: 0–8225–1507–5 (lib. bdg. : alk. paper)
    1. Bush, George W. (George Walker), 1946– —Juvenile literature.
2. Presidents—United States—Biography—Juvenile literature. I. Title.
II. Series.
E903.M373 2007
973.931092—dc22
[B]   2005031131

Manufactured in the United States of America
1 2 3 4 5 6 – JR – 12 11 10 09 08 07

CONTENTS

George W. Bush—with his wife, Laura, and daughters, Jenna (back left) and Barbara (back right). Bush and his family thank supporters following Bush's 2004 presidential acceptance speech on November 3.

INTRODUCTION

*America has spoken, and I'm humbled by
the trust and the confidence of my fellow
citizens. With that trust comes a duty to serve
all Americans, and I will do my best to fulfill
that duty every day as your President.*
—George W. Bush, during his 2004
presidential acceptance speech

On November 3, 2004, George Walker Bush thanked Americans for choosing to reelect him as the president of the United States. His previous term as president had been filled with disputes and tough decisions, including a controversial election, terrorism, and war. The 2004 reelection, however, proved that a slim majority of U.S. voters deemed him worthy for a second term as the most powerful person in the United States.

Despite family wealth, influence, and power, success had often eluded George W. Bush in his early years. He did not do well in school, was defeated in his first political race, failed at early business ventures, and battled a drinking

problem. Even after Bush managed to win his party's nomination for president in 2000, fellow Republicans questioned the way he ran his campaign against the Democratic
challenger, Vice President Al Gore of Tennessee. Although
Bush finally prevailed over Gore, he lost the popular vote
in what was probably the most disputed presidential election in U.S. history.

Before the end of his first year as president, George W.
was faced with a state of emergency. Terrorists had attacked
the United States on September 11, 2001. Bush's leadership
was tested as the country worked to recover. From that attack
sprang the global war on terror, a campaign to battle terrorists around the world and to bring peace and security to the
United States. Before his first term ended, the new president
had sent troops to invade Afghanistan and then to invade

Iraq, eventually overthrowing Iraqi leader Saddam
Hussein. Many Americans
felt the war in Iraq was
wrong and accused the

✧ —————————
*President George W. Bush
speaks to world leaders in
2002 about his vision for
defeating terrorism.*

president of misusing his power. Others supported his decision and believed the defeat of Saddam made the world a safer place.

While Bush's core supporters continue to hail his dedication to fighting terrorism, his critics take issue with the management of the war in Iraq and with the handling of domestic issues. For example, many Americans criticize the U.S. government's slow response to Hurricane Katrina, which hit the Gulf Coast in the summer of 2005, devastating New Orleans, Louisiana, Biloxi, Mississippi, and other coastal cities. With the advance warning that was available to officials, many people feel the administration should have acted more quickly to prepare for the natural disaster, evacuated people more speedily from dangerous areas, and helped citizens rebuild quickly after the storm.

Many Americans are also concerned about the constitutionality of the National Security Agency's secret monitoring of domestic phone lines without warrants—a security procedure that was secretly authorized by Bush as an anti-terrorism measure starting in 2004. Funding cuts for many educational, health care, and social programs have also caused concern about the president's domestic priorities.

As Bush's second term moves into its final years, polls show that fewer Americans than ever are confident in Bush's management of the government, his honesty, and his actions in Iraq and at home. Yet his confidence and optimism for the country continue: "I know the American people want somebody to stand on principle, make decisions and stand by them and lead this world toward a more peaceful tomorrow, and I strongly believe we're doing that. And I enjoy it. It's a fantastic opportunity."

*George H. W. Bush proudly carries his first son, George W. Bush,
on his shoulders. Family and friends called the father
and son Big George and Little George.*

CHAPTER ONE

BIG GEORGE, LITTLE GEORGE

I guess I learned in a harsh way, at a very early age, never to take life for granted.
—George W. Bush

When George W. Bush ran for president of the United States in the 2000 and 2004 elections, he liked to present himself as a "good ol' Texas boy." He was proud, he said, that he had nothing in common with the East Coast preppies (such as his opponents, Al Gore and John Kerry) whose families ran the government and the financial centers of power in Washington, D.C., and New York City.

But George W. actually had much more in common with those folks than he let on. For example, although Bush was the governor of Texas and spoke with a Texas twang, he was not a native Texan. George W. was born thousands of miles away from the Lone Star State. Little George, as he was known in childhood, was born on July 6, 1946, on the East Coast in New Haven, Connecticut. Like

Gore, whose father was a U.S. senator from Tennessee, George W. was born into a powerful political family. His grandfather was Prescott Bush, a U.S. senator from Connecticut. Other relatives were bankers and Wall Street stockbrokers. The Bush family could trace their ancestry back to fourteenth-century England, "making [George W. Bush] a fourteenth cousin to Queen Elizabeth II and a relative of the entire British royal family."

BUSH FAMILY ROOTS

In the Bush family, Big George was George Herbert Walker Bush, George W.'s father. When Little George was born, his father was finishing his education at Connecticut's Yale University after serving in World War II (1939–1945). Big George had met Barbara Pierce, a distant relative of former president Franklin Pierce, at a country club dance in Greenwich, Connecticut, in 1941. The couple became engaged two years later, in 1943, while Big George was a fighter pilot in the U.S. Navy. In 1944, while on a bombing mission, his plane was shot down. He parachuted out of the plane, landing in shark-infested waters before being rescued. A few months later, he returned home to a hero's welcome. Dressed in his navy uniform, Big George married Barbara on January 6, 1945. On his forehead was a large bandage, hiding a cut he'd received while jumping from his burning airplane.

After graduation from Yale University in 1948, Big George faced a tough choice. He could follow his father and family into the world of business and politics on the East Coast, or he could set off in a completely new direction. Big George decided to set off on his own. He moved his young

George H. W. and Barbara Bush happily pose for photographers on their wedding day in 1945.

————————— ✧

family to western Texas, where one of the greatest oil booms in history was starting. Seeking to cash in on the boom, Big George took a job as a clerk with one of the oil drilling companies in the area. He rented a small apartment in a tough neighborhood in the city of Odessa. It was all Big George could afford on a monthly salary of $375.

A year later, the company moved the family to California, where George W.'s sister Pauline Robinson (whom everyone called Robin) was born in 1949. The family returned to Texas the next year, settling in Midland, a dusty little town full of tumbleweeds and rattlesnakes, seemingly in the middle of nowhere. Midland, however, was the center of the oil boom. So big was the boom that the town soon became the richest in the country. It boasted more Rolls Royce luxury cars per person than anywhere else in the

United States. A few years after arriving, Big George started his own oil company, Zapata Petroleum Corporation, named after the famous Mexican revolutionary Emiliano Zapata. Bush decided on the name after seeing a popular movie called *Viva Zapata!* starring Marlon Brando.

CHILDHOOD

In 1950 the Bush family bought a two-bedroom home on a street nicknamed Easter Egg Row. The houses were built so much alike that the owners painted them bright colors to tell them apart. The Bush home was painted bright blue and cost seventy-five hundred dollars. Within a

✧ ———————

Little George accompanies his father at the opening ceremony for a Zapata offshore drilling platform in the 1950s. Big George moved his family to Texas, hoping to strike it rich in the booming oil business there.

couple of years, as Zapata Petroleum became more successful, the family moved to a better neighborhood and a better house, this one with a swimming pool.

Friends and relatives remember George W. as being an extremely active child. He was the class clown, always cracking jokes and wanting to be the center of attention—traits he carried with him throughout his life. Living in Midland suited young George W. He attended Sam Houston Elementary School. He passed his days swimming in the pool, riding bikes, climbing behind the bleachers at Friday night football games, playing catcher on his Little League baseball team, and attending family barbecues. Bush recalls that neighbors watched out for one another. He remembers when a friend's mother caught him crossing the street without looking both ways. The mom yelled at him as if he were her own son, then lectured him not to do it again.

"Midland was a small town with small-town values," George W. recalled. "We learned to respect our elders, to do what they said, and to be good neighbors. We went to church. Families spent time together, outside, the grown-ups talking with neighbors while the kids played ball or with marbles and yo-yos. No one locked their doors, because you could trust your friends and neighbors. It was a happy childhood. I was surrounded by love and friends and sports."

FAMILY GRIEF
But life in Midland was not without tragedy for George W. In February 1953, his sister Robin died of cancer. Robin had begun feeling ill earlier that month, about the same

time the Bush's third child, John (nicknamed Jeb), was born. Big George and Barbara decided not to tell their eldest son how seriously ill his sister had become. It was a tough choice, but as Barbara Bush said years later, "We thought he was too young to cope."

Little George discovered how serious the illness had been while at school one day. His parents, who had been in New York with Robin while she received treatment, drove to pick him up two days after his sister had died of cancer in New York. George W., who was in the second grade, was taking a record player to the principal's office with a friend when he saw his parents' car. He ran to a teacher to tell her that he had to go because his parents and sister were waiting for him. "I run over to the car and there's no Robin," Bush recalled.

It was then that his parents told him what had happened. "I was sad, and stunned," Bush later said. "I knew Robin had been sick, but death was hard for me to imagine. Minutes before, I had had a little sister, and now, suddenly, I did not. Forty-six years later, those minutes remain my starkest memory of my childhood, a sharp pain in the midst of an otherwise happy blur." In addition to the pain of losing Robin, Little George was upset that his parents had not told him how sick Robin had been. And Little George's parents also wondered if they'd done the right thing by not telling him. They said they did not want to burden him with such terrible news because there was nothing he could do. For a long time, George W., who was seven when Robin died, had nightmares about his sister's death.

Barbara Bush said later, "I don't know if that was right or wrong, but he said to me several times, 'You know, why didn't you tell me?'"

Young George W. (center) *helped lighten the mood in his family following the death of his sister, Robin, in 1953.*

———————————— ✧ ————————————

George W.'s parents also felt Robin's loss. Barbara Bush went into a depression. Her hair turned white before she was thirty years old from the strain of coping with the loss. People visiting the house, even George W.'s young friends, noticed how sad George W.'s mom had become. Eventually people did not mention Robin's name inside the Bush home.

George W. finally broke the sadness in the household and brought some needed laughter to his parents without intending to. George had just learned about how the earth spins on its axis, when one day after school, he asked his mother which way Robin had been buried in her grave.

"What difference would it make?" his mother asked him.

"One way she'd be spinning like this," he said, demonstrating by turning himself around in one direction. "And one way like this," he said, reversing direction.

Another time George W. attended a football game with his father and some of his friends. When the boy's vision was blocked by adults, he turned to his father and said he wished he were dead like his sister Robin up in heaven. After a brief silence, the father asked his son why. "I bet," Little George said smiling, "she can see the game better from up there than we can here."

CHAPTER TWO

SCHOOL DAZE

It was a shock to my system.
—George W. Bush, on life at Phillips Academy

The small-town lifestyle that George W. enjoyed in Midland changed dramatically in 1959. After serving as the seventh-grade class president and quarterback of the football team, he and his family—which now included Neil (born in 1955), Marvin (born in 1956), and Dorothy (born in 1959)— moved to Houston, one of the biggest cities in the country. George W.'s father wanted to get into politics, and he thought business and political prospects were brighter in the big city. Little George quickly made friends. He became a class officer at the private Kinkaid School and also joined the school football team. The friendships he made while in Houston were so strong that many friends stayed with him in important jobs all the way to the White House.

But an even bigger change in George W.'s young life took place in 1961, when his parents sent him away from home for the first time. George Herbert Walker Bush had graduated from Phillips Academy in Andover, Massachusetts, and he and Barbara wanted their son to follow in his footsteps. They took him on a visit to Andover and enrolled him in the private academy. The move marked a turning point in George W.'s life because he had to make his way without his family for the first time. He and his friends did not understand why he had to go away to Andover.

"'Bush, what did you do wrong?' a friend in Houston had asked, only somewhat jokingly, upon hearing I was going away to boarding school," Bush recalled. "In those days, Texas boys who got shipped off to boarding school were usually in trouble with their parents. In my case, Andover was a family tradition; my parents wanted me to learn not only the academics but also how to thrive on my own."

AT THE ACADEMY

The fact George W. was doing something for his parents and something they believed to be for his own good did not make his time at Andover any easier. "Forlorn is the best way to describe my sense of the place and my initial attitude," Bush said about arriving at Andover. "Andover was cold and distant and difficult. In every way it was a long way from home."

George W.'s stay was even more difficult because his dad was something of a legend at the school. His father had been a star athlete, a near perfect student, and president of the senior class. Upon graduating, the elder Bush had delayed going to college so he could enlist in the military, becoming the youngest pilot in the U.S. Navy in World War II. When he returned home, he attended Yale

George W. (second from left, back row) *poses with classmates for a class photo during his studies at Phillips Academy in the 1960s.*

———————————— ✧ ————————————

University—one of the country's most elite schools—and after graduation, he started his own company.

"Throughout his days, George W. would be trailed by the halo and shadow of his father," writes biographer Elizabeth Mitchell, who covered the Bush family for many years. "Some of the twinning of mannerisms could be downright spooky to friends . . . [and] of course, they shared the same first and last names. People were always doing somersaults to distinguish between the two of them." The comparisons started almost as soon as George W. arrived at Phillips.

What people at Phillips most remember about George W. was his love of stickball. Stickball, similar to baseball, is a game played in the streets of New York. A broom handle or other long wooden stick is used to bat a small rubber ball to score runs. George W. created a stickball league and got everyone on campus to join. He named himself commissioner of the league and set up a schedule of games and playoffs. George W., who was sometimes mistakenly called Junior, also played varsity basketball and baseball. He was not considered a star on the field, but he worked hard.

George W. did not do well in the classroom. In fact, he did so badly that he was afraid he was going to flunk out of

———————— ✧
Head cheerleader George W. cheers the Phillips Academy football team during a game in the 1960s. Bush also was a member of the academy's baseball and basketball teams.

school. The first essay he wrote in an English class was a complete failure. George W. misused big words he did not understand, and the teacher gave him a zero on his report. "And my math grades weren't all that good either," Bush said years later. "So I was struggling."

Although Bush never made the honor roll, he was popular on campus. He made friends easily and earned the nickname Lip because he had an opinion on just about everything and often spoke sharply. He became the head cheerleader for the football team at the all-boys school. He also was a member of a rock-and-roll band, the Torqueys. George W. didn't play an instrument. His job was to stand on stage and clap his hands. When he graduated from Phillips, he was popular enough to finish second in the election for Big Man on Campus.

COLLEGE BOUND

After graduation, Bush had to decide which college to attend. Although he did not seem to enjoy being away from home or being on the East Coast, he wanted to follow in his father's footsteps and go to Yale. Yale University is a member of the Ivy League. Ivy League schools are a collection of northeastern colleges and universities that have reputations of academic excellence and social prestige. It did not appear that George W. had the grades to get into such a distinguished school, however. George W. applied there anyway, but he also applied to the University of Texas, a good school but with less strict entrance requirements than Yale.

As critics would point out later in his life, his father and his family's connections rescued the younger George Bush.

Not only his father but also his grandfather had gone to Yale. Because he was the relative of prominent Yale graduates, George W. Bush was admitted to the university to keep the family tradition, or legacy, alive.

George W. set off for Yale in the fall of 1964 to study history. He soon found himself in the middle of history.

"George and I are both witness to the fact that Andover has such an excellent academic system, and even people at bottom tier—where I was and George was—can be okay and go to good colleges," said classmate Don Vermeil.

CHAPTER THREE

THE LAST OF THE SHORT HAIRS

We were young men trying to enjoy what should have been the last carefree days of youth.
—George W. Bush

Many Americans opposed U.S. involvement in Vietnam. Young men who weren't attending school were required to sign up for the draft. If selected, those chosen would be required to enroll in the armed forces. This put young men at risk of being sent to fight in Vietnam whether they wanted to go or not. Some refused and fled the country or were arrested. George W. arrived at Yale in 1964 during the Vietnam War (1957–1975) and at the beginning of a cultural upheaval. The radicalism, the antiwar protests, the drug use, and the alternative lifestyles that came to symbolize the 1960s were in their early stages. By the time Bush and his classmates graduated in the spring of 1968, the country had experienced dramatic changes.

George W. struggled with Yale University's elite Ivy League atmosphere during his studies there in the mid-1960s.

✧ ————————————

"We later joked that members of the class of 1968 were the last in a long time to have short hair," Bush said. Despite his ability to laugh about his time at Yale, George W. was not happy with the school. He believed Yale and many other Ivy League schools harbored what he called intellectual snobs, people who thought they were smarter than everybody else. George W. also thought the university had never given his father the respect he deserved. "I was irritated at Yale," Bush said. "I just can't believe the university would not be bending over backwards to say to one of the most distinguished alumnas *[sic]* they've had, that they're going to . . . give this man an honor and treat him with utmost respect. Maybe that's not fair to the institution for me to feel that way, but I feel that way."

THE IVY LEAGUE
George W.'s anger began soon after arriving on campus, when he met one of the leading Yale intellectuals, the

Reverend William Sloane Coffin, who had attended the school with George W.'s father. By the time George W. went to Yale, Coffin was the chaplain at Yale and a protester against the Vietnam War. George W. introduced himself to his father's old classmate just after the elder Bush had been defeated in a U.S. Senate race by Senator Ralph Yarborough, a liberal Democrat. George W. said he remembers Coffin telling him, "I know your father and your father lost to a better man."

Coffin insists that he does not remember the incident. And if it did happen, he said, he was probably kidding. "I knew he wasn't kidding," George W. said. "He might have been kidding—I just didn't pick up on his sense of humor."

George W. was deeply offended by what Coffin had said, believing the comment was a personal attack against his father. The comment not only awakened a deep desire in George W. to protect his father but it also fueled his growing dislike of Ivy League intellectuals.

"I've been turned off by intellectual snobbery most of my life," George W. has said. "Once you go to those schools and can compete academically, you realize that these people . . . really are quite shallow. Just because you've got a big university by your name doesn't mean you're any smarter or any brighter than somebody else, necessarily. It matters how you apply your education. . . . I think one of the things that people have found out about me, and maybe a lot has to do with how I was raised and who raised me, is that I am an unpretentious person."

Unassuming and unpretentious are good words to describe George W. at Yale. He wore rumpled clothes and drove an old, beat-up car. He seems to have made as little impact at Yale as he did at Andover. Most of his teachers don't remember him being involved in campus social and academic activities. Instead, George W. focused his time on intramural sports and partying. As a freshman, he was a pitcher on the Yale baseball team, and he took up rugby two years later.

DATING, DRINKING, AND DKE

While at Yale, Bush developed a drinking problem. Bush joined the Delta Kappa Epsilon (DKE) fraternity, known as the biggest-drinking, loudest-partying house on campus, geared mainly toward athletes. The fraternity brothers at DKE did some outrageous stunts and got into occasional problems with authorities. Bush, who became president of the fraternity just like his father had, was often in the middle of the pranks. One night, while walking home from a party where he had drunk too much, he suddenly laid down in the middle of the street and rolled himself home. While attending a football game at Princeton, Bush and some friends tore down the goalpost after Yale beat Princeton to win the Ivy League championship. "We charged onto the field to take the goal post down . . . the police were not nearly as impressed with our victory as we were," Bush recalled. "We were escorted off the field and told to leave town. I have not been back since."

That wasn't Bush's only brush with the law in college. During the Christmas holidays one year, in what Bush describes as "the infamous Christmas wreath caper," police arrested Bush and some friends for stealing a wreath from a local store. Bush claims the group was "liberating" or borrowing the wreath. He was charged with disorderly

Many of George W.'s classmates at Yale thought of him as a good-time guy. But others disapproved of his drinking and sometimes wild behavior.

✧ ──────────

conduct, but the charge was eventually dropped after Bush and the others apologized for what they had done.

Friends say that while Bush had a wild side as a young man, he never did anything bad enough to prevent him from one day becoming president of the United States. In fact, they say, most of the things that Bush got involved with can probably be blamed on a combination of too much alcohol and not enough maturity.

"George was a fraternity guy," said Calvin Hill, a DKE brother who went on to play professional football with the Dallas Cowboys. "He [Bush] went through that stage in his life with a lot of joy, but I don't remember George as a chronic drunk. He was a good-time guy. But he wasn't the guy hugging the commode at the end of the day."

G. W. AND DKE

When George W. Bush joined Delta Kappa Epsilon (DKE), the fraternity was more than one hundred years old. It was organized in 1844 at Yale University after the two original fraternities Alpha Delta Phi and Psi Upsilon refused to accept some prominent members of the younger class. In protest, other students and initiates created DKE. Membership criteria included "equal portions the gentleman, the scholar, and the jolly good fellow." Since its creation, five members of DKE have become U.S. presidents, including both George W. and George H. W. Bush, Gerald Ford, Rutherford B. Hayes, and Theodore Roosevelt.

When George W. decided to become a pledge for DKE, he joined fifty other young men hoping to be accepted into the fraternity. At one point, the older members tried to embarrass the new pledges by challenging them to name all fifty-five pledges. Most of the initiates could only remember five or six names, but when it was his turn, George W. was able to recite the name of every single pledge. By the time he was a senior, George W. had been elected DKE president.

DKE was recognized as one of the loudest fraternities on campus. George and his fraternity brothers were soon well known for their wild antics. During the winter holidays of his junior year, George and a few of his friends were arrested for trying to steal a Christmas wreath. George also, on one occasion, literally rolled home after a night of drinking. As DKE president, George W. continued to abide by the rules of "the jolly good fellow." One frat brother remembered DKE as being much like the fraternity in the movie *Animal House*, commenting that George would have been played by Jim Belushi's character, Bluto, who was the wildest and most fun-loving of the group.

Campus and public opinion of the frat was not always accepting. In 1967 DKE was accused of abusing its pledges by branding them with a piece of metal shaped into the house's insignia. DKE members claimed that the branding practice was more of a psychological test than a physical one. Prior to the branding, the pledges were shown a four-inch, red-hot steel brand. As they turned around, the iron was replaced with something smaller. The injury, according to George W., who was later quoted in an article by the *New York Times*, was no more than "a cigarette burn." While some alumni recalled not enjoying the experience, many others, including Bush, considered it an important DKE tradition.

Friends recall Bush as being popular but going on only a few dates. He did get into some serious trouble with his father because of a girl, however. One summer while in college, George W. got a job on an oil rig in the Gulf of Mexico. He was dating a girl in Houston and missed being with her. Since he would be heading back to college soon, he wanted to spend more time with her. So he quit his job and returned to Houston to be with her. His father was not amused. He called George W. into his Houston office and told his son how disappointed he was with the choice the young man had made.

George W. broke up with that girl a short time later but eventually found a new romance. During the Christmas break of his junior year at Yale, Bush got engaged to Cathryn Wolfman, a student at Rice University in Houston. Bush was twenty, the same age his father had been when he'd become engaged. However, George W.'s engagement to Wolfman ended quietly the following year as the couple drifted apart.

While college students across the country were marching for civil rights and against the Vietnam War, the most serious controversy Bush engaged in during his time at Yale was the fraternity's practice of "branding" pledges who wanted to join DKE. Bush and his fraternity brothers used a piece of heated metal to burn, or brand, the skin of prospective members. When the practice became public in 1967, it created a national story. In a much-publicized article in the *New York Times*, Bush defended the practice by saying the branding wounds were no worse than cigarette burns.

Although George W. was far different from his father at Yale, he did follow the elder Bush in one respect: joining

The Skull and Bones Society meetinghouse at Yale University. George W.'s grade point average was below that set for membership. But the elite student group accepted George because his father was once a bonesman.

──── ✧ ────

the secret Skull and Bones Society on campus. His father had been a famous baseball player and war hero when selected to join the elite group. Each year the group chose and accepted the top fifteen Yale students. Although George W. was not among them, he was allowed to join Skull and Bones as a legacy. He was allowed his membership to maintain the family tradition. Bonesmen are sworn to secrecy about what takes place during their meetings, but some members have talked anonymously to journalists over the years. While many members agonized about what they would do when drafted, what they remember about Bush is how passionately he defended his father, who supported the Vietnam War.

"MILITARY SERVICE OR NOT"

While George W. spent his time partying at Yale without a care in the world, the world began to nudge him and his fraternity brothers during their senior year. In 1968 the Reverend Martin Luther King Jr. was assassinated, as was New York senator Robert Kennedy a few months later. The killings left many college students saddened and angry. Meanwhile, more and more U.S. soldiers were dying in Vietnam as the war escalated in Southeast Asia.

"The events of 1968 rocked our previously placid world and shocked the country, Yale, and me," Bush recalled. "In many ways that spring was the end of an era of innocence. The gravity of history was beginning to descend in a horrifying and disruptive way."

———————— ✧
U.S. soldiers carry a wounded member of their division out of heavy fighting during the Vietnam War in the late 1960s.

By the time George W. graduated with a degree in history, he and his friends had to confront the Vietnam War head on. "The war was no longer something that was happening to other people in a distant land; it came home to us," Bush said. "We didn't have the luxury of looking for a job or taking time to consider what to do next. We were more concerned with the decision that each of us had to make: military service or not."

Thousands of young men faced with such a tough decision decided to leave the United States and head to Canada to avoid the draft. Bush, whose father was by then a congressman, said he never considered such a decision. "I knew I would serve," Bush said. "Leaving the country to avoid the draft was not an option for me; I was too conservative and too traditional. My inclination was to support the government and the war until proven wrong, and that only came later."

Bush, however, found a way to serve without being sent to Vietnam. He joined the Texas Air National Guard. Bush applied in Houston and was accepted almost immediately. The enlistment proved a very controversial decision for both the National Guard and the future presidential candidate.

George W. Bush during his service in the Texas Air National Guard during the Vietnam War. Bush and other privileged sons chose to enlist in the Guard, avoiding the draft and active combat in Vietnam.

CHAPTER FOUR

THE WILD BLUE YONDER

I served, and I am proud of my service.
Yet I know it was nothing comparable to what
our soldiers and pilots were doing in
battle in Vietnam.
—George W. Bush

The enlistment of George W. Bush in the National Guard was bound to draw attention, and it did. In joining the Guard, George W. followed the sons of many prominent families in Texas. These young men had found a way to perform their military service without risking their lives in combat. The Guard was a reserve group stationed in the United States. The Guard also flew older jets and other aircraft, so even if the unit was called to Vietnam, it probably would not fight.

Later, the media questioned whether George W. had received preferential treatment. They wondered whether being a congressman's son allowed George W. to leapfrog over more deserving candidates. Congressman Bush's district included the Houston area, where George W. had signed up. Also, George W. had scored the lowest acceptable grade on the pilot aptitude test, much lower than other more qualified candidates had done on the entrance exam. Later, a concern was raised about the fact that Bush had not filled out the section on the application asking about past illegal activity.

George W.'s response to all the criticism was that he had probably just forgotten to fill in the illegal activity section of the application. He denied that Texas politicians and friends of his father pulled strings to get him accepted. The enlistment required two years of training and four years of part-time duty. Bush said most men didn't want to be in the military that long, so there were fighter-pilot openings in the Guard. He insisted that he would have gone to Vietnam if ordered to do so. Bush said he chose the Guard not to avoid combat but because it was the quickest way to become a military pilot like his father.

"I was well aware of my dad's service as a navy fighter pilot in World War II . . . I'm sure the fact that my dad had been a fighter pilot influenced my thinking," Bush said. "I remember him telling me how much he loved to fly, how exhilarating the experience of piloting a plane was. I was headed for the military, and I wanted to learn a new skill that would make doing my duty an interesting adventure. I had never flown an airplane but decided I wanted to become a pilot."

But according to Bush biographer Elizabeth Mitchell,

> *while the pilot training and Air National Guard*
> *service that followed were by no means easy,*

George W. receives his second lieutenant bars from his father during a promotion ceremony in the 1960s. Bush's acceptance into the Guard and his promotion were highly publicized.

---

pleasant experiences, they were a far cry from being sent into the infantry. . . . That meant that George W. got exactly the military situation he was looking for, an uncommon luxury in that era.

Regardless of how Bush got into the Guard, the unit commander, Colonel Walter B. "Buck" Staudt, made sure everyone in Houston knew about it. Bush was sworn in on the same day he applied, but Colonel Staudt held a special ceremony weeks later so journalists could photograph him with the congressman's son. When George W. was later promoted to lieutenant, Staudt held another ceremony for the newspapers. This time Staudt invited Congressman Bush, who flew from Washington to Houston to be photographed with his son and the colonel.

The attention continued. As the political career of George W.'s father advanced, people also noticed his eldest son. Congressman Bush had campaigned for Richard Nixon in Texas during the 1968 presidential race. When elected,

Nixon had rewarded the congressman by appointing him to several important political posts. Critics say that because of this relationship, George W. was allowed to do things other servicemen could not. A few months after enlisting, for example, George W. was allowed to take a two-month leave to work for a Republican candidate in Florida. The next year, while George W. was still in training, President Nixon sent a special air force plane to Georgia, where Bush was stationed, to fly the young man to Washington for a date with his daughter Tricia.

THE "NOMADIC" YEARS

The high-profile date with the president's daughter gave George W. a reputation as a lady's man. Like other pilots,

In 1969 President Richard Nixon flew Bush to Washington,
D.C., for a date with the president's daughter Tricia (above).

George W. was known as someone who liked to work hard and play hard, a lifestyle that only intensified as Bush went on weekend, or part-time, duty in 1970 after graduating from training school on June 23. Having so much free time was not a good thing for George W. The next two years of his life got even wilder as he entered what he called his irresponsible, or nomadic, years. During this time, his life drifted without direction.

Bush was one of the most eligible bachelors in Texas, and he seems to have enjoyed that reputation. The twenty-four-year-old Bush rented a one-bedroom apartment in a Houston complex that was popular with singles. He played all-day games of pool volleyball with other residents in one of the complex's six swimming pools.

In 1971 President Nixon named the elder Bush to be the U.S. representative to the United Nations in New York. The United Nations is an international organization that was created in 1945 to promote international peace, security, and economic development. The Bush family moved to New York, but George W. stayed in Houston. A family friend, Robert Gow, hired George W. to work at Stratford of Texas, a Houston-based company that sold agricultural products. It was the first nine-to-five, coat-and-tie job George W. had ever held, and he hated it. He stayed there only about nine months.

Then George W. toyed with the idea of running for the Texas legislature. His family name was well known in Houston, and the newspapers soon heard about his plan. The *Houston Post*, among others, wrote a story about the younger Bush wanting to get into politics, erroneously identifying George W. as George Bush Jr.

Meanwhile, President Nixon asked the elder Bush to become chairman of the Republican National Committee, one of the most important political jobs in the United States. In 1973 the Bush family moved to Washington, D.C. After spending the fall in Alabama to work on the campaign of Winton "Red" Blount, a conservative Republican running for the U.S. Senate, George W. went to visit his family at Christmas. While there, he got into a drunken confrontation with his father that helped the young man find some direction.

——————————— ✧ ———————————

George H. W. Bush (front right) *joins President Nixon* (front center) *and others during a Republican campaign rally in the early 1970s. While the elder Bush's political career was taking off, George W. struggled to find direction.*

The argument began after George W. took his sixteen-year-old brother, Marvin, out drinking. George W. was driving home when he ran over a neighbor's garbage can. The can stuck under the car, but George W. kept driving, producing a terrible racket. When he pulled up to his parents' house, the elder Bush awoke to find out what was going on. He naturally became upset when he saw what condition his sons, the car, and the garbage can were in. An argument followed between George W. and his father. At one point, George W. even challenged his father to a fight. The elder Bush was able to calm George W. down, but the incident troubled him. He began to think about what his son should do next.

After quitting his agricultural sales job, George W. had decided to return to school to get his graduate degree. He wanted to become a lawyer and had applied to the University of Texas Law School, but his application was rejected. He then applied to Harvard Business School, one of the most prestigious schools in the country. But, if accepted, George W. would not start classes until September, more than nine months away. After their fight, the elder Bush was worried that his son might get into more trouble. He arranged to have George W. do community work in one of Houston's poorest neighborhoods.

LIFE EXPERIENCES

George W. was hired as a counselor in the Professional United Leadership League (PULL). PULL had been started by John L. White, a former Houston Oilers football player, to provide mentors to inner-city minority kids. The program helped teenagers seventeen and under by providing them with counseling and recreational programs. The kids played sports, learned arts and crafts, and hung out in an old warehouse that the organization owned. George W. was a counselor in the program, and during the summer of 1973, Marvin Bush joined his older brother. They were the only white people working in the building. "They stood out like sore thumbs," said Muriel Simmons Henderson, another counselor. "John White was a good friend of their father. He told us that the father wanted George W. to see the other side of life. He asked John if he would put him in there."

George W. proved a huge success with the kids and his coworkers. He wrestled with the kids, played basketball with them, and took them on field trips. George W. found it easy to relate to the children because in many ways he was still a big, fun-loving kid himself. Coworkers remember Bush driving around in a beat-up old car. Bush had so many clothes and papers in the car that no one else could fit inside it. "He was a super, super guy," said Ernie Ladd, a former professional football player and professional wrestler. "If he was a stinker, I'd say he was a stinker. But everybody loved him so much. He had a way with people."

The experience also made quite an impression on George W. He recalls the sadness he felt at seeing how hard the lives of the kids were. On one occasion, a boy no more than eleven or twelve years old was playing basketball with George W. When the child jumped to shoot the ball, a loaded pistol fell out of his pocket. The child thought he needed the gun for protection.

George also remembers befriending a boy named Jimmy, who became like a little brother to him. Each day the boy waited for George W. to arrive and then followed him everywhere. One day Jimmy showed up at the center without shoes, so George bought him a pair. He recalls that when he walked the boy home, Jimmy's mother was high on drugs. "Jimmy was happy to be home, but I was incredibly sad to leave him there," Bush said.

"My job gave me a glimpse of a world I had never seen. It was tragic, heartbreaking, and uplifting all at the same time. I saw a lot of poverty. I also saw bad choices: drugs, alcohol abuse. . . . I saw children who could not read or write and were way behind in school. I also saw good and decent people working to try to help lift these kids out of their terrible circumstances," Bush said.

HARVARD UNIVERSITY

While at PULL, Bush received notice that he had been accepted to Harvard. He was enjoying his work with the kids so much that he thought about staying with the program, but John White convinced him to go to Harvard. "If you really care about these kids as much as I think you do, why don't you go and learn more and then you can really help," White told Bush.

Bush arrived at Harvard looking for some direction in his life. "I had learned to fly jets and acquired a good education," Bush recalled. "I had not yet settled on a path in my life." Harvard is a place where many of the future business leaders of the country were taught. But the twenty-seven-year-old Bush looked nothing like the son of a famous politician. Bush arrived at the school driving his dumpy car and sporting his usual casual clothes and attitude. In one famous yearbook photo, George W. is shown sitting at the back of a classroom, dressed in a badly wrinkled shirt, casually chewing gum and blowing a large bubble.

Despite the casual attitude, George W. took his studies seriously. He learned about finance, marketing, and other things needed to run a business. He graduated with his master's degree in business administration and then surprised many people when he followed the path his father had taken twenty-five years earlier. George W. loaded up his car and drove west to the oil fields of Texas to make his fortune.

CHAPTER FIVE

OIL'S WELL THAT ENDS WELL?

*It's hard not to take a political loss personally,
after all, it's your own name spelled out there on
the ballot. Yet if you believe in the wisdom of the
voters, as I do, you get over the disappointment,
accept the verdict, and move on.*
—George W. Bush, on his 1978 congressional loss

Although his father had been in the oil business, George W. had no experience running an oil company. He had his master's degree in business administration from Harvard, but George W. started at the bottom and worked his way up.

In 1975 George W. started out by working as a land man, looking up records in county courthouses around Texas to see who owned what properties. He then tried to get the owners to lease or sell the land to a company drilling for oil. George W.'s engaging personality served him well. He was able to drive up to homes and start conversations with complete strangers.

At about the same time, Bush decided to run for Congress in the 1977 race. He had worked on some of his father's races, so he had a good idea of what was involved in running a campaign. A popular Democratic congressman from the area had decided to retire unexpectedly. Bush, seeing a chance to win the seat for the Republicans, decided to run in the Republican primary—an election to choose which candidates from a particular party will run in the general election. His father was delighted that his eldest son was following the family traditions and entering politics. George W.'s family and friends, including Joe O'Neill and Don Evans, were eager to help. Karl Rove, who had worked for George W.'s father, also went to Midland to help. Neil Bush, who had recently graduated from college, joined the campaign too.

LOVE AND POLITICS

In August, the same month George W. announced his congressional candidacy, Joe O'Neill and his wife, Jan, invited him to a barbecue. There, George W. met Laura Welch, a quiet elementary school librarian with no interest in politics. The unlikely couple was attracted to each other and went out the following night to play miniature golf. George took Laura to Houston, Texas, in October to meet his family. And less than three months after meeting each other, on November 5, 1977, George and Laura were married at the First United Methodist Church in Midland. "If it wasn't love at first sight, it happened shortly thereafter," Bush said about meeting his wife. "My wife is gorgeous, good-humored, quick to laugh, down-to-earth, and very smart. I recognized those attributes right away in roughly that order."

George W. and Laura Bush (center) on their wedding day in 1977. They are joined by family members (from left to right): Marvin, Dorothy, Neil, Columb (Jeb's wife), Jeb, Barbara, George, and Dorothy Walker Bush.

——————— ✧ ———————

Shortly after the wedding, George W. went back to his campaign but promised Laura that she would not have to make any speeches. A few months later, however, a terrified Laura made her first campaign speech in Muleshoe, Texas. In June 1978, George won the Republican primary election and began his campaign for the November general election.

The general election against Kent Hance, George W.'s Democratic opponent, proved to be educational. Despite Bush's prior experience, he was not prepared for the Hance campaign. Hance painted the younger Bush as an outsider to Texas, pointing out that Bush had been born in Connecticut and had gone to school back East at Phillips, Yale, and Harvard. Hance said that his own father and grandfather had been farmers in Texas for decades before the Bush family showed up. Hance easily won the election.

After the lost election, Bush decided to get back into the oil business. He started his own oil drilling company, which he called Arbusto—Spanish for "bush" or "shrub." Family friends helped him start the company, raising millions of dollars to buy equipment, lease offices, and hire workers. According to former workers, he treated people

George W. campaigns with Laura for his election to the U.S. Congress in 1978. Bush lost the race to his Democratic challenger, Kent Hance.

fairly and stayed out of the way of the technical people who actually decided where to drill for oil. Bush and his company enjoyed some success while the price of oil remained relatively high in the early 1980s.

BIG GEORGE'S VICTORY

In 1980 George took a break from business to devote himself to his father's primary campaign for the Republican nomination for president. The elder Bush had decided to enter the Republican primary to try to defeat incumbent president Jimmy Carter in the general election. Carter, a peanut farmer and former governor from Georgia, had become unpopular partly because of the economic problems the country was experiencing—such as oil shortages, high gasoline prices, inflation, and high unemployment. Adding to the problem, sixty-six U.S. citizens had been taken hostage by Iranian terrorists on November 4, 1979. More than a year later, fifty-two were still being held at the U.S. Embassy in Iran. Unsuccessful attempts to free the hostages weakened Carter politically and made him vulnerable in the 1980 presidential election.

Although the elder Bush did not win the Republican nomination for president, the eventual nominee, Ronald Reagan, did select him as his vice-presidential running mate. In the November general election, the Reagan-Bush ticket won the presidency.

George W. and Laura attended the presidential inauguration in January 1981. When his father took the oath of office as vice president of the United States, George W. was filled with pride. He felt that same emotion the following November, when Laura gave birth to twin daughters. The happy parents named the girls Jenna Welch, for Laura's mother, and Barbara Pierce, for George W.'s mother.

Meanwhile, George W. began thinking about getting back into a political race himself. He considered running for governor of Texas, which surprised his family. They wondered if he had the necessary experience for such a high office. Barbara Bush even told her son that he was probably not ready to run for the governor's office. One of her concerns was that it was too soon after George H. W.'s victory, and having a famous father could work against

——————————— ✧ ———————————

George H. W. Bush (front left) is sworn in as vice president in 1981. Barbara Bush (center) warned G. W. to hold off on returning to politics because having a powerful father could actually hurt his chances.

George W. during the campaign. George W. was angry, but he wisely listened.

"ALL NAME AND NO MONEY"

Instead of going into politics, George W. devoted himself to keeping his oil company in business. George W. was not as successful as his father had been, and by 1982 the oil industry began to go into a slump. In 1984 Bush merged Arbusto with a larger oil exploration company called Spectrum 7. By 1985 the price of oil had gone from $25 to $9 per barrel. Companies and fortunes were wiped out. George W.'s company was among those suffering in West Texas. The company was on the verge of bankruptcy. Bush was once again rescued by his name and family connections. "I'm all name and no money," George W. was heard to say while looking for someone to bail out his company.

The rescuer was a big company named Harken Energy Corporation. The company wanted to use the Bush name and George W.'s family connections. So Harken bought Spectrum 7 in 1986 and paid off the company's $3.1 million in debts. Harken also hired many of the former Spectrum employees. Bush was hired as a consultant for $120,000 a year while he was working full-time on his father's presidential campaign in the late 1980s. He also received $300,000 of Harken stock and was made a member of its board of directors.

"What was Harken getting for its money? The son of the vice president of the United States," the founder of Harken answered when asked how the deal helped Harken. "His name was George Bush. That was worth the money they paid him."

When the Harken deal closed, Bush was able to walk away with hundreds of thousands of dollars and the possibility of making much more than that through a stock plan. Although George W. was finally set financially, he once again had fallen short. Just as he had tried and failed to follow in his father's footsteps at Andover and Yale, George W. again failed to reach the kind of success his father had enjoyed in the oil business. But George W. did gain something from his failure in the oil business. The business deal helped set him up for his next big venture: the world of professional baseball.

CHAPTER SIX

HIGHBALLS AND HARDBALLS

From baseball, I developed a thick skin against criticism. I learned to overlook minor setbacks and focus on the long haul. I would find those skills invaluable in my campaigns.

—George W. Bush

Before George W. moved up to the major leagues, he had to deal with a major problem—his excessive drinking. The drinking had been bothering him and his family most of his adult life. When drinking, George W. often lost his temper, got into arguments, and said things that weren't as funny as he thought. On one occasion, George W. berated the *Wall Street Journal* writer Al Hunt, swearing at him in public. He frequently arrived at work hung over from the previous night's binge. Although Bush insists he was not an alcoholic, he also readily admits that he had a bad habit of drinking too much and then getting into arguments.

*Bush asserts that he decided to quit drinking at the age of forty
during a stay at the Broadmoor Hotel* (above) *in 1986.*

———————————— ✧ ————————————

That all changed when, at the age of forty, Bush decided
that enough was enough.

Laura had been trying to get her husband to quit
drinking for years, and a conversation with the Reverend
Billy Graham, a family friend, got Bush seriously thinking
about making this life-altering decision. But it wasn't until
the celebration of his fortieth birthday that Bush finally
decided to quit. George W., Laura, and some friends gathered at the Broadmoor Hotel in Colorado in June 1986 to

celebrate several birthdays. The next morning, Bush, an avid runner, went out for his usual jog. He felt so terrible that he decided his body was trying to tell him he was getting too old to drink. He decided to stop and claims he hasn't had a drink since.

"There are turning points in life, and one of mine was quitting drinking, which I finally did shortly after my fortieth birthday. My wife and friends later joked that . . . I quit after seeing the bar bill," said Bush, who says it was not difficult to stop. "People later asked if something special happened, some incident, some argument or accident that turned the tide, but no. I just drank too much and woke up with a hangover."

THE "ENFORCER"

After deciding to refrain from alcohol, Bush was faced with another tough decision. No longer working on a daily basis, he was once again looking for something to do with his life. In 1986 he joined his father's presidential campaign as an adviser. The elder Bush, after eight years of being vice president, was finally getting his chance to run for president in 1988. George W. served as his father's "enforcer" on the campaign trail. He insisted on complete loyalty to his father from the entire campaign staff and often got into yelling matches with workers and journalists. He did so because he was obsessed with making sure that campaign workers were loyal to his father and that journalists were fair about what they wrote about him. But these arguments fueled his growing reputation of having a bad temper.

He became especially angry when witty Ann Richards of Texas, the keynote speaker at the Democratic National

Convention, portrayed the elder Bush as a weak politician who succeeded only because he had had things handed to him his whole life. She also poked fun at his habit of mispronouncing words. During her speech on national television, Richards said it really wasn't his fault. "Poor George," she said, "he can't help it. He was born with a silver foot in his mouth." The memorable remark drew a huge laugh from the audience, but it also upset the Bush family, especially George W.

Despite his temper, people acknowledged that George W. was a hard worker who played an important role in getting his father elected to the presidency of the United States. His father's election victory made George W. better known

—————— ✧
Ann Richards addresses the 1988 Democratic National Convention. During her speech, Richards made some comments questioning George H. W.'s ability to speak and lead that angered George W. He became his father's election campaign enforcer, defending George H. W. to the media.

around the country. Once again George W. toyed with the idea of getting into politics, possibly running for governor of Texas. He and his advisers decided a 1990 race would be too close to his father's election. Although George W. and his family occasionally visited the White House, George W. consciously distanced himself from his father by not getting involved politically or getting appointed to any agency in his father's government. For most of his life, George W. had been fighting the perception that he had gotten where he was because of his father. If George W. was to have any political future, he needed to do something to establish himself, so he decided to jump into the world of professional baseball. With a group of other men, he became part owner of the Texas Rangers.

HARKEN STOCK

George W. had always been a huge fan of Major League Baseball. As a child, he had collected baseball cards, memorized statistics, and pretended to be Willie Mays, his favorite player. George W. obtained the money for his part of the Rangers purchase by taking out a bank loan, using his Harken stock to guarantee the loan. In 1990 Bush sold 212,140 shares of that stock to pay off the loan. But the stock sale proved controversial. He sold the stock on June 22, 1990, when the company's stock price was $4 a share. Bush made $835,000 on the sale. Within two weeks, the stock price dropped to less then $2.50 a share.

The obvious question was whether Bush, who was on Harken's board of directors, had known about the financial problems before they became public. If so, had he sold his stock based on that information to avoid the drop in stock

price that would surely follow?
This type of selling, called insid-
er trading, is illegal. A com-
plaint was lodged against Bush,
and the Securities and Exchange
Commission (SEC) investigated.
This federal agency enforces the
laws governing the purchase and sale of stocks and bonds.

George W. said he had not known about the company's
financial difficulties. He insisted that he would not have
sold the stock if he had known about the problems. He
pointed out that Harken's lawyers had studied the sale and
said it was okay. Bush also maintained that he hadn't found
out about the financial problems until a month after he
sold the stock. The government finally ended its investigation in 1993, deciding there was not enough evidence to
charge Bush with any crime.

OWNING A BASEBALL TEAM

With his money secured, Bush and a group of friends
bought the Texas Rangers, a team that had never had much
success. The team played near Dallas, and their biggest star
was the legendary pitcher Nolan Ryan. Bush's political

advisers thought the purchase was a good move because it made Bush a famous Texas businessman. If Bush was serious about entering the 1994 Texas governor's race, being with the club would keep his name in the news on an almost daily basis.

Bush's part of the purchase price was $600,000. Once again, his primary benefit to the other investors was his name and family history. The group purchased the team for $75 million in 1989. Bush was given a 10 percent stake in

Part owner of the Texas Rangers, George W. mugs for reporters, stepping on his father's stomach during the president's pre-jog warm-ups.

the team and was asked to serve as the team's public spokesman and managing partner. The most significant thing the group did was to get a new $190-million stadium built in 1994. This greatly increased the value of the team and helped Bush prove that he could come through on a major project.

The job with the Rangers also helped the people of Texas to get to know George W. He had his mother, then the First Lady, throw out the first pitch at a Rangers' game. He spoke to community groups about the team every week and was in the stands for each home game. He signed thousands of autographs for fans and even got his boyhood dream fulfilled when the team issued a baseball card with his picture on it. While he was with the Rangers, Bush suffered only two big setbacks: the Rangers never won the World Series, and he was unsuccessful in getting his father reelected president. Bill Clinton defeated the elder Bush in 1992 by 43 percent to 38 percent of the vote.

CHAPTER SEVEN

THE CANDIDATE

*People ask me if I have any concern for what
this will do to my family. My answer is that
my concern for them is why I am here.*
—George W. Bush, on running for governor
of Texas

In 1994 some of George W.'s friends believed that one of
the reasons he decided to run against Ann Richards, who
had been elected governor of Texas in 1990, was to get
back at her for her popular 1988 joke about his father.
"Ann made a name for herself and her tongue in 1988 by
ridiculing my father," Bush said. "She built on that attention to mount a successful campaign for governor in 1990.
But if she wants a second four-year term, her biggest road-
block is going to be another George Bush."

Despite being well known around the country and in
Texas because of his identification with the Rangers, George
W. realized he would have to be careful in his race against

Richards. She was a popular governor, the most popular in
thirty years. Richards also had a great sense of humor,
which she displayed on television with talk-show hosts such
as Jay Leno and David Letterman. Bush advisers feared that
with her quick wit, Richards would make George W. so
angry that he would embarrass himself. Bush and his people also knew that the biggest problem George W. faced
was being seen as just another George Bush.

"My biggest problem in Texas is the question, 'What's
the boy ever done? He could be riding his Daddy's name,'"
Bush said prior to the campaign. George W. decided to
address the issue directly. He told his parents to stay away
from the press conference at which he announced his candidacy so they would not be the focus of attention. At his
first campaign stop, he stated his reason for running for
governor. "I am not running for governor because I am
George Bush's son," he said. "I am running because I am
Jenna and Barbara's father." Although George W. didn't let
his father get involved in his campaign, his mother campaigned for him and for his brother Jeb, who was running
for governor of Florida that same year.

GOVERNOR OF TEXAS

George W. Bush ran on the issues of reforming the welfare
system, toughening the juvenile justice system, and decen-
tralizing public education, which promoted state funding of
schools versus using local property taxes. He also played it
smart throughout the campaign. As much as he disliked Ann
Richards, Bush decided that the best way to defeat her was
to be nice to her. "We're never going to attack her because
she would be a fabulous victim," Bush told his advisers.

Ann Richards (left of TV screen at right) *and George W. debate during the 1994 gubernatorial race in Texas. Bush, a seeming underdog in the race, went on to win the election.*

———————————— ✧ ————————————

"We're going to treat her with respect and dignity. This is how we are going to win." Bush didn't even show anger when Richards said George W. had gotten everything in life because of his father. Bush only criticized Richards's policies.

The formula proved successful. Bush surprised many people around the country and won the election with 53 percent of the vote. Richards managed to get only 46 percent. Suddenly, George W. Bush was the governor of one of the biggest states in the country, and he was seen in a new light.

George W. (right) *receives congratulations from his father* (left), *wife Laura* (center), *and others during his gubernatorial inauguration in 1995.*

———————————— ◇ ————————————

George W. quickly became a major national political force. All he had to do to remain a Republican power broker was to avoid doing anything foolish in office so people would continue to take him seriously. His brother Jeb, however, was not so lucky. Jeb lost the governor's race in Florida that year.

The entire Bush family gathered in Texas to see George W. get sworn in as governor. They had reason to be proud. George W. was the first Republican to be elected governor of Texas since 1877. George, Laura, and the twins moved to Austin, Texas, to live in the stately governor's mansion.

George W. proved to be an effective, but not spectacular, governor. He focused on harsher penalties for criminals, local control of education, cutting welfare, protecting corporations from big lawsuits, and other issues. He made no major blunders while in office. As a result, many Republicans began to consider Bush as a possible presidential candidate for 1996, after only two years in office. What made the possibility enticing was that George W. would face Bill Clinton, the man who had defeated his father in 1992.

Although George W. decided against running in 1996, he remained the Republican favorite for the year 2000. This became especially true after Bush won reelection in Texas in 1998, becoming the first governor in the history of Texas to win two four-year terms in a row. He had learned how to appeal to both the moderate and the conservative wings of the Republican Party.

————————————✧

Bush waves to supporters during his gubernatorial reelection celebrations near the Texas Capitol Building in 1999.

Governor Bush on Education and Crime

When George W. became governor of Texas, the Texas Assessment of Academic Skills (TAAS) revealed that more than 350,000 school children could not pass the minimum skills reading test. Education was one of the many issues George vowed to address as governor. After learning of the results, Bush created the Texas Reading Initiative, which set a goal that all students should be literate by the third grade.

His education program held schools responsible for failing students. Students were required to take the TAAS test to determine if the schools were successful. Schools whose students repeatedly failed or showed little improvement were at risk of losing their federal funding. "I am a strong advocate of accountability. I believe in results." Bush explained, "If you don't measure how students are doing in school, how do you know whether teachers are teaching and students are learning?"

As governor, Bush encouraged parents to send their children to different schools if their children weren't learning at their current school. Bush also argued in support of federal funds for charter schools. He believed that parents and educators should do whatever was necessary to teach students to read. He brought many of these proposals into his presidency. In 2002 he signed the No Child Left Behind Act, which applied many of these guidelines to the entire U.S. education system.

Another issue Bush felt was important during his term as governor was juvenile crime. Bush began work on the juvenile justice system immediately upon his election. During the 1995 legislative session, Texas strengthened its juvenile justice laws. In the past, juvenile offenders had hours of free time and were

Many Texans did not like George W.'s affirmative stance on the death penalty and sharply criticized the rising number of executions while he was governor.
───────── ✧

allowed to wear their own clothes. After the 1995 session, offenders were issued orange uniforms and their days were strictly regimented. Bush said, "Discipline and love go hand-in-hand . . . we must teach young people there are bad consequences for bad behavior if we hope to change their bad choices." Bush explained that the strict lifestyle within the system would discourage new and repeat offenders. Bush also tripled the number of beds in juvenile detention facilities, which created more room and allowed the courts to assign longer sentences for violent juveniles. Bush encouraged legislators to pass a bill that would lower the age at which a minor could be tried as an adult. His proposals also affected adult prisons.

During his campaign, Bush had announced that he would end parole for the most violent adult offenders. The plan was thrown out, however, because parole is considered a basic human right under the U.S. Constitution. Nonetheless, in the adult jail system, Bush appointed a stern parole board. The new board cut parole approvals by 8 percent. During Bush's two terms as governor, Texas was successful in lowering its crime rate and juvenile crime had the first decline in decades.

That same year, his brother Jeb won the Florida race for governor. In George W.'s victory speech, he congratulated Jeb and described himself as a "compassionate conservative"—a term that would serve him well.

Perhaps in preparation for a run at the White House, Bush and his partners decided to sell the Texas Rangers after George W. was reelected. They sold the team in 1998 for $250 million. As his part of the profits, Bush got almost $15 million. He was set financially for life.

He could now focus on seeking the Republican nomination for president in 2000, a point not lost on his friends and political advisers. "Congratulations," Bush's friend Joe O'Neill told him after the sale. "You hit the long ball. Now you can run for president. . . . You're free."

RUNNING FOR PRESIDENT

In April 1998, Bush attended a private meeting at Stanford University. Leading Republican thinkers, economists, and foreign policy experts wanted to meet Bush to see if he had what it took to be president. They asked him questions about taxes, foreign policy, Social Security, terrorism, and other issues.

Bush was understandably nervous. He realized that in many ways he was auditioning for the group, and his future might well depend on his performance. After many hours of questioning, Bush passed the test. The group thought he was pleasant, intelligent, and asked good questions. Bush himself seemed surprised at how well the meeting had gone. Leaving the meeting, he joked with one of his advisers that the group "didn't seem to think I was slobbering on my shoes."

Bush announces his candidacy for the 2000 presidential election. Bush and his campaign staff understood that they were in for an especially tough fight to win the presidency.

Soon prominent Republicans by the dozens made their way to Austin, Texas, to meet Bush. They not only brought their good wishes but also money and the ability to raise more money. By the time Bush officially announced his candidacy, he had attracted more than $15 million to spend on the upcoming primaries. Eventually, he and national Republicans raised more than $350 million for the 2000 presidential election.

Bush and his advisers believed they would need every penny of it to win. The country was at peace. The economy was doing well, and the likely opponent, Vice President Al

Gore, had much more government and campaign experience than Bush did. But before Bush could campaign against Gore, he had to win the nomination of his own party. And while this hurdle initially seemed easy due to his popularity and campaign funding, it got much more difficult when a strong Republican challenger emerged.

CHAPTER EIGHT

THE RACE FOR THE WHITE HOUSE

I am running hard, and I am running to win.
—George W. Bush

George W.'s Republican opponent for the nomination was Senator John McCain of Arizona. McCain was a war hero who caught people's attention. During the Vietnam War, McCain had been held prisoner for about five years. He had been tortured so much that he couldn't raise his arms above his head. McCain looked like a father figure compared to Bush's frat boy image. Unlike Bush, who liked to repeat his simple message over and over, McCain liked to deliver his speech and then engage people in spontaneous conversation. In his campaign bus, called the Straight Talk Express, McCain traveled the country trying to overtake Bush's huge lead and financial advantage. In the first primary, held in New Hampshire on February 1, 2000, Bush lost to McCain.

The New Hampshire defeat took the wind out of Bush's sails. Many of the doubts people had had about Bush began to resurface. The media referred to Bush as Dubya, a play on both his middle initial and his Texas drawl. People wondered if George W. had enough political experience and if he was smart enough to campaign against someone as mature as John McCain. For a few tense weeks, people wondered if Bush would crack under the pressure, but he remained calm. He didn't fire anybody on his staff. He did not change his message. He kept his sense of humor.

Bolstered by a pep talk from Laura, who urged him to be himself and be more aggressive in fighting for the nomination, Bush headed to South Carolina for the next primary. He defeated McCain in what turned out to be a nasty and controversial primary. The controversy arose after twenty-one polling stations did not open and many people were unable to vote. The candidates also attacked one another with negative campaign ads. By the end of March, Bush was clearly in the lead. The road was now open for him to be nominated the Republican candidate for president. During the Republican National Convention in Philadelphia, his parents watched with pride as he accepted the nomination.

PUBLIC SCRUTINY AND DOUBT

As the campaign got in high gear, George W. faced his harshest criticism. The news media questioned Bush's apparent lack of intelligence, his lack of experience, and his casual attitude. Reporters started writing about how Bush seemed to smirk, as if he were always joking. Another writer who did a profile of Bush even speculated that Bush might be dyslexic or have another learning disability.

Bush denied any problem, but people wondered just how smart he was. Most of all, people wondered whether Bush was mature enough to be president. Not only was Gore extremely intelligent, he was, in some ways, the complete opposite of the fun-loving Bush.

Bush countered some of these concerns by surrounding himself with smart advisers who generally made a good impression when dealing with the public and the press. He also picked Dick Cheney as his choice for vice president. Cheney, a former congressman from Wyoming, had served as the elder Bush's secretary of defense during his presidency.

This selection focused attention on another big issue raised against Bush: how much George W. had benefited from his father's name and accomplishments.

——————— ✧

Presidential candidate George W. Bush (far right) and his vice-presidential running mate Dick Cheney on the campaign trail in 2000. Bush surrounded himself with political veterans and smart advisers to dispel concerns about his intelligence and ability to lead as president.

"That George W. Bush has traded on his father's name all his life is observably true," said Molly Ivins, a Texas columnist who covered Bush when he was governor of that state. "In fact, one could argue that he's never really done anything else."

George W. responded to these criticisms by saying he was very proud of his father but that he was his own man. He acknowledged he had learned a lot from his father, but it was mainly about how to be a good husband and father.

Bush also had to guard against doing or saying anything outrageous enough to upset people or further call his abilities

———————— ✧ ————————

Bush makes fun of attacks on his intelligence in 2000. Media and critics continued to question the candidate's ability to lead a nation.

and qualifications into question. For example, the Bush campaign was accused of subliminally flashing the word *RATS* in a commercial aimed against Democrats. Afterward, Bush was mocked when he mispronounced the word *subliminal* when responding to criticism of the ad. People also laughed at Bush when he called the citizens of Greece "Grecians" instead of Greeks. At one campaign stop, he had asked the crowd, who were listening to him talk about education reform, "Is our children learning?" Bush was widely ridiculed for these mishaps. In fact, as the campaign wore on, comedians—from David Letterman and Jay Leno to the players on *Saturday Night Live*—made more and more jokes about the candidates. For the first time in election history, comedians were taken seriously by the candidates and the voters. In fact, people were paying so much attention to the comedians that both Bush and Gore found it necessary to go on some of the comedy shows themselves to prove that they could take a joke.

DEBATES AND THE ELECTION CONTROVERSY

One of the major obstacles that Bush faced was a series of debates held a few weeks before election day. Bush's casual attitude and his apparent lack of intellect led some journalists to wonder how well Bush would do against Gore. Gore was considered to be one of the best debaters in the country. Before the debates, people speculated that if Bush lost the debates or appeared to be ignorant, he would lose the election.

To the surprise of many people, Bush held his own against Gore. Bush was seen as a nice man who knew enough. He seemed relaxed, cheerful, friendly, and hopeful about the future. Bush survived the debates by sticking to his message, not arguing with Gore, and constantly repeating the same phrases over and over again. Once Bush avoided the pitfalls of the debates, it appeared he stood a good chance of becoming the next president.

The vote for president proved to be one of the most controversial in U.S. history. It was not settled until thirty-five days after the November 7 vote. The controversy centered on Florida, where George W.'s younger brother Jeb was the governor. Problems with counting the votes delayed a final decision on election night. At first, the media declared that Gore had won the state. Then it appeared that George W. had won. Whoever won Florida's twenty-five electoral votes would win the election. In the days that followed, both parties went to court. The Florida Supreme Court wanted a recount in questionable counties, which probably would have favored Gore. But the U.S. Supreme Court ordered the counting to stop, with Bush ahead by a few hundred votes. George W. Bush had finally secured his place in history. He would be the forty-third president of the United States.

But even after Bush was declared the winner, threats to his success still existed. His victory might be challenged in Congress, or one or more of the electors in the electoral college might switch camps and vote for Gore. The tense situation finally calmed down when Gore went on national television and said Bush would be the next president. In a short speech, Gore asked that people support the new president. In response, Bush promised to be president to everyone in the United States and to unite what had become a deeply divided country.

Legal disputes over ballot counting in states such as Florida left the 2000 presidential election undecided for more than one month. In the end, Bush narrowly defeated Democratic challenger Al Gore.

——————————— ✧ ———————————

THE NEW PRESIDENT

As a freezing rain fell on Washington, D.C., George W. Bush was sworn in as the forty-third president of the United States on January 20, 2001. The inauguration officially ended all doubt about the outcome of the presidential election, but the unusual circumstances of the election left a cloud hanging over Bush's victory.

Bush had to deal with the anger generated by his election victory. During the campaign, Bush had promised the country that he would be a uniter and not a divider. After Bush took the oath of office, he had to make good on that promise by giving the most important speech of his life.

ELECTORAL COLLEGE

Although people in the United States think they are directly electing the president when they vote, they are not. People are actually voting for the electors who will later vote for president. Sound confusing? It can be, but blame the confusion on the Founding Fathers, who created the electoral college. Members of the electoral college decide who becomes president of the United States.

Many people who vote probably aren't even aware of the electoral college. That's because members of the electoral college usually do their job routinely and without controversy. But sometimes controversy erupts and people question what the electoral college is and why it has such power. The electoral college is a group of people who gather once every four years in late December to elect the president. That is why they are called electors.

The electoral college was created in 1787 during the Constitutional Convention in Philadelphia because the Founding Fathers could not agree on the best way to elect a president. Some wanted a popular vote while others favored having Congress select from among the candidates. The electoral college was seen as the best compromise.

How are the electors selected? Indirectly, by the voters. Each state has a specific number of electors, or electoral votes, equal to the size of its congressional delegation: its two senators plus its members of the House of Representatives. The number of electoral votes ranges from three in states such as Vermont to fifty-five in California. Most state electoral votes usually go in a winner-take-all format to whichever presidential candidate gets the most votes from registered voters in that state. That means that if a candidate loses in a large state, even by one vote, he does not get any electoral votes from that state. If he loses enough big states, that candidate could not win even if he wins all the smaller states because he would not get enough electoral votes to win. That is why a candidate can lose the popular vote but still win the electoral vote and become president. That is what happened in the 2000 election between George W. Bush and Al Gore. Gore won the popular vote 50,996,116 to 50,456,169. Bush won the electoral college 271 to 266, with one voter casting a blank ballot. It was the fifth time in U.S. history that a candidate won the popular vote but lost the presidency.

Electors, however, are free to vote for whomever they want. Although there are some state penalties for being what is called an unfaithful elector, there is no federal law or anything in the Constitution that requires electors to vote for the candidate that won their state. Such switching has only happened about nine times. Most people don't switch because they are loyal to their party and its candidate. Only electors of the state's winning party vote in the electoral college. Switching votes, however, was a big concern of the Bush camp in the 2000 election. Not only was the electoral vote close, which meant every vote was crucial, but Gore had won the popular vote. Bush supporters were worried that some electors might have thought this situation was unfair and vote for Gore. That did not happen, however, and Bush won the vote of the electoral college.

Over the years, more than seven hundred attempts have been made to abolish or reform the electoral college, but the smaller states have defeated these proposals. If candidates only had to win the popular vote, they would spend all their time campaigning in cities and states with the highest populations. They could then ignore smaller states because they would not have enough voters to justify the amount of time spent campaigning there. The electoral college system at least ensures that the voices of the smaller states are heard.

During his inaugural address in 2001, Bush speaks of the importance of uniting the nation after the highly divisive 2000 election.

———————— ✧ ————————

Unification was, indeed, the main theme of George W.'s inauguration speech. As millions watched on television and hundreds of friends and family stood nearby, Bush made a solemn pledge to "work to build a single nation of justice and opportunity. I know this is within our reach." Bush also promised to restore civility, respect, and responsibility to the presidency while creating what he called a compassionate country and government. After Bush finished his speech, supporters gathered on the Capitol steps cheered as a band began playing the traditional song reserved only for the president of the United States, "Hail to the Chief."

Even as the music was playing, however, thousands of protesters chanted and yelled in the streets of Washington,

D.C. The demonstrations were the first major protests on inauguration day since 1973, when Richard Nixon was sworn in while tens of thousands protested the Vietnam War. The anti-Bush demonstrators, while fewer in number, still required the tightest security ever for a presidential inauguration. Police officers stood every few feet along the inauguration parade route as protesters voiced displeasure not only about Bush's stand on civil rights and abortion but also about his being selected (by the Supreme Court) and not elected to the presidency. One sign held aloft in the crowd during the televised inaugural parade seemed to sum up their feelings. It proclaimed, Hail to the Thief.

—————————— ✧ ——————————

While Bush delivered his inaugural address, demonstrators protested his controversial election to the U.S. presidency.

Some Electoral History

As wild, dramatic, and nerve-racking as the 2000 presidential election was for the country and the world, it was not unique in U.S. history. In fact, the race between George W. Bush and Al Gore was the fifth time that a candidate had become president by losing the popular vote and winning the electoral vote.

The first time was in 1800, when it took several days and thirty-six ballots in the House of Representatives for Thomas Jefferson to be selected president over Aaron Burr. The two candidates were tied in the electoral college with seventy-three electoral votes each from the nineteen states then in the Union. Since no clear winner emerged in the electoral college, election rules required the House of Representatives to determine the next president. The vote finally swung in Jefferson's favor when Alexander Hamilton, who hated Burr, convinced enough representatives to vote for Jefferson. Burr, who never forgave Hamilton, carried a grudge for many years. In 1804 Burr challenged Hamilton to a duel, in which Hamilton was shot and killed.

The next contested election, in 1824, did not lead to bloodshed, although emotions ran equally high. The electoral college selected John Quincy Adams, whose father had been the second president, over Andrew Jackson. Jackson, a famous general, had won the popular vote and also was ahead after the first vote in the electoral college. But Henry Clay, who was not only a candidate but also the Speaker of the House, made a deal with Adams. Clay urged the representatives to support Adams. In return, Adams would name Clay his secretary of state. Jackson got his revenge when he defeated Adams for the presidency in 1828.

Things were quiet for the electoral college for more than fifty years. Then, in 1876, a decade after the Civil War

(1861–1865), another presidential election crisis erupted. Democratic governor Samuel J. Tilden of New York won the popular vote over Republican Rutherford B. Hayes of Ohio. Tilden seemed to be on his way to victory when several southern states, still upset over their defeat in the Civil War, conspired to snatch the victory away from him. Democratic ballots were thrown out in Louisiana, South Carolina, and Florida because of supposed fraud, violence, and intimidation against black voters. Republican officials "threw out" the votes in counties with especially bad records of violence and fraud. When these votes were thrown out, Hayes carried the three states. In a scene that was repeated 124 years later, both candidates sent lawyers to Florida to file lawsuits contesting the vote. After the disputes were settled, the electoral count ended up in a tie. Congress set up a commission of eight Republicans and seven Democrats to select the winner. The Republicans voted as a group, and Rutherford B. Hayes was selected as the seventeenth president of the United States— just three days before his inauguration.

In 1888 the most popular candidate again did not become president. Grover Cleveland, who was running for reelection, was able to get ninety-one thousand more popular votes than his challenger, Indiana senator Benjamin Harrison. But Cleveland lost in the electoral college by a large margin, 233 to 168. Harrison was declared the winner, despite widespread charges of fraud by Cleveland's supporters. Although several close presidential elections occurred in the years that followed, most notably in 1948 when Harry Truman beat Thomas Dewey and in 1960 when John Kennedy beat Richard Nixon, it was not until the new millennium when Bush beat Gore that history repeated itself.

The controversy over the election hurt Bush in a couple of ways. It focused attention away from George W.'s remarkable transformation from being an irresponsible youth to being the most powerful man in the United States. Also, instead of focusing all of his attention on delivering on his campaign promises of cutting taxes and improving the education system, Bush knew he would have to expend a lot of energy to convince people that he was the true president of the United States.

"Expectations in this country [are] we can't get anything done," Bush said at a luncheon with congressional leaders on

inauguration day. "People say, 'Well, gosh, the election was so close, nothing will happen except finger-pointing and name-calling and bitterness.' I'm here to tell the country that things

✧ ───────────────

President Bush continued his message of unification during an address to a joint session of the House and Senate in February 2001.

will get done, that we're going to rise above expectations, that both Republicans and Democrats will come together to do what's right for America."

With those words, George W. began his role as the president of the United States. He was the first president elected in the new millennium—which seemed fitting in light of the historic nature of his election and the great debates that it inspired.

Only nine months into his presidency, George W. Bush was confronted with an unprecedented national tragedy—the September 11, 2001, terrorist attacks on the Pentagon and the World Trade Center.

CHAPTER NINE

A PRESIDENT TESTED

The safety of the American people depends on ending this direct and growing threat. Acting against the danger will also contribute greatly to the long-term safety and stability of our world.
—George W. Bush, on the occupation of Iraq

As a new president, George W. Bush focused on many things, such as education reforms, Social Security, and medical care. But these issues soon fell to the wayside as a more demanding problem appeared. On September 11, 2001, terrorists attacked the United States. Two hijacked airplanes were flown into the World Trade Center in New York, while a third crashed into the Pentagon near Washington, D.C. A fourth plane crashed into a vacant field near Pittsburgh, Pennsylvania, never reaching its target. Nearly three thousand people were killed in the attacks. As the American people struggled with a multitude of emotions, their focus soon turned to the new president. President Bush addressed

A U.S. soldier stands behind an Osama bin Laden wanted poster at Ground Zero in New York City in 2001. Bush called for the capture of bin Laden and other terrorists responsible for the 9/11 attacks. He would expand the hunt to a general war on terrorism.

✧ ————————————

their fears with confidence and determination. "The search is underway for those who are behind these evil acts. I've directed the full resources of our intelligence and law enforcement communities to find those responsible and to bring them to justice." Soon the hijackers were identified as members of the terrorist group al-Qaeda. Al-Qaeda was based in Afghanistan and led by a Saudi Arabian man, Osama bin Laden.

In October, President Bush executed Operation Enduring Freedom, a campaign that sent U.S., British, and local Afghan troops deep into Afghanistan to destroy al-Qaeda terrorist training camps and capture terrorist leaders there. President Bush had begun what he called the war on terror.

He felt it was his duty to protect the United States and the American way of life. Terrorists, he explained, wanted to destroy what the United States and other freedom-loving countries valued. By December the war against terror was largely considered a success, as the remaining al-Qaeda strongholds fell. Bin Laden, however, had not been found.

OCCUPATION OF IRAQ

The following year, President Bush continued his war on terror by targeting Iraqi leader Saddam Hussein. Bush's father and the United Nations had defeated Saddam during the Gulf War in 1991, and afterward, the Iraqi leader had agreed to end developments for weapons of mass destruction (WMD).

———————— ✧

George W. took his war on terrorism to Iraq, declaring war on the nation and its leader, Saddam Hussein (right), in 2003. While Bush argued Saddam held WMD and was a source of world terrorism, many wondered if the president wanted to finish the job his father started in the 1990s.

Remembering September 11

Following the attacks on September 11, 2001, the Pentagon began planning a memorial. The project was sponsored by the Department of Defense and run by the U.S. Army Corps of Engineers. In June the following year, the Army Corps of Engineers requested entries for its design competition. The winning design would be installed near the location where the hijacked plane hit the Pentagon.

There were more than two thousand entries in the United States alone. The winning design was created by Julie Beckman and Keith Kaseman. Their design included 184 memorial benches in honor of the people who lost their lives during the attack on the Pentagon. All the benches are angled lengthwise to match the direction that the plane flew into the building. Each bench contains the name of a single victim, and the benches are arranged according to the victims' ages. The ages, ranging from three to seventy-one, are also acknowledged on an "age wall" that divides the memorial from the nearby road. Beneath each memorial bench is a reflecting pool that is lit from the bottom after dusk. The Pentagon memorial was scheduled to be completed in the fall of 2006.

The memorial competition for the Ground Zero site

9/11 attack, New York City

attracted more than five thousand proposals. The winning design, created by Michael Arad, is called Reflecting Absence. The design emphasizes the absence left behind after the destruction of the World Trade Center towers.

Instead of building skyward, Arad created two pools in the "footprints" of the towers. The underground space can be accessed by two ramps that lead visitors more than thirty feet beneath the surface. There, the pools are continuously filled by a cascade of water that runs down the stone walls of the memorial. Inscribed around the pools are the names of each victim of September 11 and the 1993 bombing.

Connecting the two pools is a single tunnel that doubles as an area for visitors to leave candles and other memorials. The tunnel also contains a large chamber for memorial services. On the surface, the memorial is surrounded by a city plaza and rows of eastern pines. The memorial at New York City's Ground Zero is scheduled to open in 2009.

After 9/11, however, President Bush said he received information that not only did Saddam have WMD, but he also had harbored known al-Qaeda terrorists. Saddam denied these accusations but refused to allow U.N. inspectors into certain areas within Iraq. President Bush asked the United Nations to intervene and remove what he said was a threat to the United States. "We cannot stand by and do nothing while dangers gather. We must stand up for our security, and for the permanent rights and the hopes of mankind. By heritage and by choice, the United States of America will make that stand. And, delegates to the United Nations, you have the power to make that stand, as well."

Bush soon found, however, that some delegates in the United Nations refused to support his plan of overthrowing the Iraqi leader. French and Russian delegates proposed new, less aggressive resolutions that allowed Saddam more time to work with inspectors. Seeing that the United Nations would not support him, President Bush took matters into his own hands. He did not believe he needed the permission of the United Nations to act. On March 19, 2003, President Bush announced that war had begun in Iraq. "My fellow citizens, at this hour, American and coalition forces are in the early stages of military operations to disarm Iraq, to free its people and to defend the world from grave danger."

Many in the United States and around the world disagreed with Bush's decision. They thought he should have waited until he had received the United Nations' support. Some believed he wanted to overthrow Saddam because he wanted to control the rich oil fields in Iraq. Others thought Bush was trying to prove that he was as capable as his father, who had led the United Nations coalition against Saddam in

An unidentified U.S. soldier removes Saddam Hussein from a crude bunker near his hometown of Tikrit, Iraq, on December 13, 2003.

1991. Still, his supporters felt that as the president of the United States, he had the right to protect his country. The information the president was receiving convinced him that removing Saddam from power was the only way to ensure the safety of the United States.

On December 13, 2003, U.S. troops found Saddam Hussein in a hole near his hometown of Tikrit, Iraq. Saddam surrendered, and images of his capture were broadcast all over the world. Many of those people who originally protested the war were happy to see the Iraqi dictator removed from power. Though many Iraqi people celebrated the removal of the former president, Saddam's supporters continued to fight. The following month, the public was informed that no WMD had been found in Iraq and prewar intelligence had been incorrect. Then, in June of 2004, the 9/11 commission concluded in its report that no credible evidence existed that Iraq and al-Qaeda cooperated on the September 11 attacks.

WEAPONS OF MASS DESTRUCTION

Weapons of mass destruction are weapons that can cause widespread damage and death. WMD kill and injure indiscriminately and are sometimes difficult to control. They include biological, chemical, radiological, and nuclear weapons.

Biological warfare is often called germ warfare. This type of warfare has been practiced for centuries and uses bacteria and viruses as weapons. These weapons can spread illnesses and diseases among humans, such as smallpox and anthrax. They can also be used against crops and livestock. Poisoning water supplies or introducing contaminated objects to groups of people are also types of germ warfare. Vaccines are available, but many illnesses can still be fatal if not treated promptly or if the bacteria and viruses have been altered to resist treatment.

Radiological weapons dispense radioactive material. Often called dirty bombs, these weapons contain radioactive materials that make people sick, causing health problems such as cancer. Radiological weapons can also destroy environments and make them uninhabitable. Usually, radiological weapons are not used if an army wants to move into enemy territory.

Chemical weapons have been used since World War I (1914–1918). Unlike biological weapons, which can take longer to infect the victims, some chemical weapons can injure or kill the victim in minutes. Chemical weapons include herbicides, poison gases, and any substance that can kill or temporarily disable a target. Chemical weapons are divided into categories depending on their use and method of attack. Some include choking agents (to attack the respiratory system), nerve agents or nerve gas (to disrupt nerve functions), and burn agents (to cause severe burning on exposed areas of the body). Chemical weapons usually come in gaseous form and can be dispersed by the wind. This

Soldiers test their chemical suits during the early occupation of Iraq in 2003. To date, no WMD have been found in Iraq.

makes them difficult to control. Most chemical weapons can be avoided with gas masks and protective gear. Some chemicals, however, are powerful enough to break through protective clothing and equipment.

The most powerful weapon of mass destruction is a nuclear weapon. A nuclear weapon is powered by the nuclear reactions of fission (splitting of an atom's nucleus) or fusion (the combining of nuclei). These reactions produce huge amounts of energy. The world saw the effects of nuclear warfare when the United States dropped nuclear bombs on Hiroshima and Nagasaki, Japan, in 1945 to end World War II. When the bombs detonated, heat energy and radiation killed more than 120,000 people. Others suffered and died from radiation that affected them years after the bomb had been dropped.

Democratic presidential hopeful John Kerry (left) and incumbent George Bush (right) campaign during the 2004 presidential election.

SECOND PRESIDENTIAL ELECTION

After the two main rationales for waging war on Iraq were found to be unfounded, many people assumed this spelled defeat for Bush in the 2004 presidential campaign. Elections were fast approaching, and even some supporters were questioning the validity of the war. Bush remained optimistic, promising a free Iraq and the end of terrorism. His opponent in the race was Massachusetts senator John Kerry, a Vietnam War veteran. Democrats and war protesters rallied behind Kerry, who criticized the president for rushing into the war in Iraq without a plan to win the peace and a clear exit strategy. President Bush's supporters were not swayed by the antiwar protests. They felt the capture of Saddam was a major historical achievement and argued that the Bush administration was working with the United Nations to help the Iraqis hold a countrywide election.

Still, on November 2, 2004, the world watched closely as American votes were tallied. President Bush gathered with Laura, Jenna, and Barbara, as well as other family members and friends. Many people assumed this election would be just as difficult as the last. However, the following day, Americans knew that George W. Bush had been reelected by another slim margin of voters. He had finally accomplished what even his father couldn't—he had defeated a strong Democratic opponent to stay in office for a second four-year term. Bush supporters, family, and friends celebrated the victory. During his acceptance speech, President Bush declared, "The campaign has ended, and the United States of America goes forward with confidence and faith. I see a great day coming for our country and I am eager for the work ahead." He knew that the following four years would be filled with important decisions, and he had a large task ahead of him.

An Iraqi woman makes a finger-stained peace sign on January 30, 2005. The dye on her fingers (which is purple) shows that she has just voted in the country's first free election in more than five decades.

CONCLUSION

*My fellow citizens, the dangers to our country
and the world will be overcome. We will pass
through this time of peril and carry on the work
of peace. We will defend our freedom. We will
bring freedom to others and we will prevail.*
—George W. Bush, on the conflict in Iraq, 2003

The Bush administration had a proud moment in Iraq on
January 30, 2005. On that day, the Iraqi people held the
first nationwide free election in more than fifty years, voting into power an interim government. Despite fear of violence from terrorists and from Saddam loyalists, the
election and others that followed that year proceeded
peacefully and received an even higher turnout rate than
most U.S. presidential elections. It seemed that the U.S.-
led military effort to bring freedom and democracy to Iraq
had succeeded.

However, Iraq's elected government is struggling. A dramatic and sustained increase in violence reflects a country
on the brink of civil war. Many U.S. officials are pushing

for military withdrawal, which the majority of Americans—
once strongly in favor of the war in Iraq—have come to
support.

The war in Iraq is not the only event that will mark
Bush's presidency. When Hurricane Katrina struck the Gulf
Coast in August 2005, tens of thousands of residents in
New Orleans, Louisiana, and other Gulf communities were
stranded in the flooded communities for days and weeks
after the storm. Many Americans, as well as the U.S.
Congress, have criticized the administration for its slow
response in the aftermath of the devastating storm.

Bush's administration and the Republican party have also
endured numerous scandals. Karl Rove and "Scooter" Libby,
top aides to President Bush and Vice President Cheney,
came under investigation in 2005 for illegally revealing the
identity of an undercover CIA agent. Many speculated that
the information was leaked to discredit the agent's husband,
a critic of the administration's Iraq policies. In 2006 Jack
Abramoff, a high-powered Republican lobbyist and close
friend of former House Majority Leader Tom Delay, pleaded
guilty of fraud and conspiracy to bribe public officials. And
while on a hunting trip, Vice President Cheney accidentally
shot a fellow hunter with pellets he was aiming at a quail.
The man fully recovered, but the incident reflected poorly
on the vice president's office.

Additionally, Bush's exertion of presidential power has
come under serious scrutiny in relation to a directive he
gave after the September 11 terrorist attacks. In his directive, Bush authorized the U.S. government to monitor
domestic communications between U.S. and foreign parties
without court-issued warrants. The administration argues

President Bush waves to White House staff and reporters as he boards the Marine One presidential helicopter. Despite facing a growing number of challenges, Bush remains confident in his leadership.

──────────── ✧

that a post–9/11 resolution authorized the program, but its legality remains uncertain.

In his second term, Bush has also left his mark on the U.S. Supreme Court. To fill the seats left open by the death of Chief Justice William Rehnquist and the retirement of Justice Sandra Day O'Connor, Bush appointed John Roberts, Jr., to replace Rehnquist and Samuel L. Alito to replace O'Connor. Many Americans wonder if Roberts and Alito, who are both conservative in their legal thinking, will affect long-held decisions on previous cases—such as the legalization of abortion in *Roe v. Wade.*

It is unclear how history will view Bush's two terms as president. While some may recall an irresponsible boy who came to power because of his father, others will remember him as the man who protected his country and liberated the Iraqi people. Either way, President Bush continues to lead the United States with decisiveness and dedication. "Our nation has defended itself, and served the freedom of all mankind. I'm proud to lead such an amazing country, and I'm proud to lead it forward."

TIMELINE

1946 George W. Bush is born on July 6 in New Haven, Connecticut.

1948 The Bush family moves to Texas.

1953 Bush's sister Robin dies from cancer.

1961 Bush is sent to Phillips Academy in Andover, Massachusetts.

1964 Bush is accepted into Yale University. He joins the Delta Kappa Epsilon (DKE) fraternity and has trouble with alcohol.

1968 Bush graduates from Yale University with a degree in history and enlists in the Texas Air National Guard. Martin Luther King Jr. and New York senator Robert Kennedy are assassinated.

1970 Bush graduates from the Air National Guard training school.

1971 George W.'s father, George H. W. Bush, is named the U.S. representative to the United Nations.

1973 Bush works as a counselor for the Professional United Leadership League (PULL). The Bush family moves to Washington, D.C. Bush is accepted into Harvard.

1975 Bush begins working in the oil industry.

1977 Bush runs for Congress. Bush marries Laura Welch.

1978 Bush wins the Republican primary election. He loses the election to Democrat Kent Hance. He starts his own oil drilling company, Arbusto.

1981 George H. W. Bush is inaugurated as vice president. George W. Bush's daughters, Barbara and Jenna, are born.

1986 Bush's Arbusto company merges with Harken Energy. Bush gives up drinking. He works as an adviser for his father's presidential campaign.

1988 George H. W. Bush is elected U.S. president.

1989 Bush is part owner of the Texas Rangers baseball team.

1992 George H. W. Bush loses the presidential election to Democratic challenger Bill Clinton.

1994 Bush is elected governor of Texas.

1998 Bush is reelected as Texas governor.

2000 Bush is elected U.S. president.

2001 Terrorists destroy the World Trade Center towers in New York City and also strike the Pentagon near Washington, D.C., using hijacked passenger jets. U.S. Operation Enduring Freedom begins in Afghanistan.

2002 Bush and the United Nations are unable to agree on whether to invade Iraq.

2003 Bush declares war on Iraq. Iraqi leader Saddam Hussein is captured.

2004 Bush is reelected as president of the United States.

2005 Iraq holds its first free election. Insurgent attacks and bombings continue, resulting in the deaths of Iraqi citizens and Iraqi and coalition military personnel.

2006 Bush's presidential approval rating falls to the lowest of any president (less than 37 percent) amid domestic scandals and the deterioration of the situation in Iraq. As the conflict in Iraq continues—surpassing the three year mark—the country hovers on the brink of civil war.

SOURCE NOTES

7 "President Bush Thanks Americans in Wednesday Acceptance Speech," *The White House,* November 3, 2004, http://www.whitehouse. gov/ news/releases/2004/11/ 20041103-3.html (October 12, 2005).

9 "Despite Polls, Bush Says He Has 'Capital,'" March 1, 2006, http:// www.cnn.com/2006/ POLITICS/ 02/28/bush .interview/index.html (April 2006).

11 George W. Bush, *A Charge to Keep* (New York: William Morrow, 1999), 15.

12 J. H. Hatfield, *Fortunate Son: George W. Bush and the Making of an American President* (New York: Soft Skull Press, 2000), 5.

15 Bush, 18.

16 George Lardner Jr. and Lois Romano, "Tragedy Created Bush Mother-Son Bond," *Washington Post,* July 26, 1999, A-1

16 Ibid.

16 Bush, 14.

16 Lardner and Romano, "Tragedy," A-1.

18 Elizabeth Mitchell, *W: Revenge of the Bush Dynasty* (New York: Hyperion, 2000), 34.

18 Ibid.

18 Lardner and Romano "Tragedy," A-1.

19 Bush, 20.

20 Ibid., 19.

20 Ibid.

21 Mitchell, 15.

23 George Lardner Jr. and Lois Romano, "Bush: So-So Student but a Campus Mover," *Washington Post,* July 27, 1999, A-1.

24 Ibid.

25 Bush, 49.

25–26 Ibid., 46.

26 "In His Own Words: 'Leadership Comes in All Forms,'" *Washington Post,* July 27, 1999, A-11.

27 Lardner and Romano, "So-So Student," A-11.

27 "In His Own Words," A-11.

27 Ibid.

28 Bush, 47.

28 Ibid.

29 Lardner and Ramano, "Bush: So-So Student," A-1.

30 "A Brief History of DKE," *Delta Kappa Epsilon,* n.d., http://www. dke.org/H2.htm (October 2005).

31 Hatfield, 34.

34 Bush, 48.

35 Ibid., 50.

35 Ibid.

31 Bush, 55.

38 Mitchell, 106.

38–39 Bush, 50–51.

44 George Lardner Jr. and Lois Romano, "At Height of Vietnam, Bush Picks Guard," *Washington Post,* July 28, 1999, A-1.

44 Ibid.

45 Bush, 59.

45 Ibid., 58.

45 Ibid., 59.

45 Ibid., 58.

47 "New Worlds: Politics, Poverty, and the Oil Business," *George W. Bush,* November 2004, http://usinfo.state.gov/products/ pubs/bush43rdp/new.htm (October 17, 2005).

48 Bush, 79.

53 George Lardner Jr. and Lois Romano, "Bush Name Helps Fuel Oil Dealings," *Washington Post,* July 30, 1999, A-1.

53 Daniel Cohen, *George W. Bush: The Family Business* (Brookfield, CT: Millbrook Press, 2000), 25.

55 Bush, 197.

57 Ibid., 132–133.

58 Hatfield, 82.

63 Ibid., 124.

63 Ibid. 123–124.

64 Cohen, 30.

64 Hatfield, 124.

64–65 George Lardner Jr. and Lois Romano, "Bush's Move up to the Majors," *Washington Post*, July 31, 1999, A-1.

68 Bush, 70.

69 Ibid., 211–212.

70 Lardner and Romano, "Bush's Move Up," A-1.

70 Evan Thomas, et al., "The Favorite Son: Pumping Iron, Digging Gold, Pressing Flesh," *Newsweek*, November 20, 2000, 51.

73 Bush, 241.

76 Molly Ivins and Lou Dubose, *Shrub: The Short but Happy Political Life of George W. Bush* (New York: Random House, 2000), xix.

77 Ronald Kessler, *A Matter of Character: Inside the White House of George W. Bush* (New York: Sentinel, 2004), 127.

82 Melinda Henneberger, "The Inauguration: The Speech; In His Address, Bush Lingers on a Promise to Care," *New York Times*, January 21, 2001, 13.

86–87 Nick Anderson, James Gerstenzang, and Doyle McManus, "Bush Vows to Bring Nation Together," *Los Angeles Times Online*, January 21, 2001, http://www.latimes.com (2005).

89 "President Discusses the Future of Iraq," *The White House*, February 26, 2003, http://www.whitehouse.gov/news/releases/2003/02/20030226-11.html (October 12, 2005).

89–90 "Statement by the President in His Address to the Nation," *The White House*, September 11, 2001, http://www.whitehouse.gov/news/releases/2001/09/20010911-16.html (October 12, 2005).

94 "President's Remarks at the United Nations General Assembly," *The White House*, September 12, 2002, http://www.whitehouse.gov/news/releases/2002/09/20020912-1.html (October 12, 2005).

94 "President Bush Addresses the Nation," *The White House*, March 19, 2003, http://www.whitehouse.gov/news/releases/2003/03/20030319-17.html (October 12, 2005).

99 "President Bush Thanks Americans, *The White House*, November 3, 2004.

101 "President Bush Addresses the Nation," *The White House*, March 19, 2003.

103 George W. Bush, "Bush Vows to Unite the Country," *FoxNews.com*, 2006, http://www.foxnews.com/story/0,2933,137486,00.html (April 2006).

SELECTED BIBLIOGRAPHY

Anderson, Nick, James Gerstenzang, and Doyle McManus. "Bush Vows to Bring Nation Together." *Los Angeles Times Online.* January 21, 2001. http://www.latimes.com (2005).

Bush, George W. *A Charge to Keep.* New York: William Morrow, 1999.

Cohen, Daniel. *George W. Bush: The Family Business.* Brookfield, CT: Millbrook Press, 2000.

Fineman, Howard, and Martha Brant. "The Test of His Life." *Newsweek,* December 25, 2000/January 1, 2001.

Hatfield, J. H. *Fortunate Son: George W. Bush and the Making of an American President.* New York: Soft Skull Press. 2000.

Ivins, Molly, and Lou Dubose. *Shrub: The Short but Happy Political Life of George W. Bush.* New York: Random House, 2000.

Mitchell, Elizabeth. *W: Revenge of the Bush Dynasty.* New York: Hyperion, 2000.

"The Presidency Shrinks Further." *New York Times,* January 19, 2001. http://www.nytimes.com (January 26, 2001).

Sanger, David E. "Momentous Challenges as Bush Reaches for 12 Minutes of Inaugural Fame." *New York Times.* N.d. http://www.nytimes.com (January 20, 2001).

Sheehy, Gail. "The Accidental Candidate." *Vanity Fair,* October 2000.

Thomas, Evan, et al. "The Favorite Son: Pumping Iron, Digging Gold, Pressing Flesh." *Newsweek,* November 20, 2000.

FURTHER READING AND WEBSITES

Anderson, Dale. *Saddam Hussein.* Minneapolis: Twenty-First Century Books, 2004.

Benson, Michael. *Bill Clinton.* Minneapolis: Twenty-First Century Books, 2004.

Bolstad, Stacy Taus. *Iraq in Pictures.* Minneapolis: Twenty-First Century Books, 2004.

Bush, Barbara. *Barbara Bush: A Memoir.* New York: Scribner's, 1994.

Bush, George H. W. *All the Best, George Bush: My Life in Letters and Other Writings.* New York: Scribner's, 1999.

Bush, George W. *A Charge to Keep.* New York: William Morrow, 1999.

Dershowitz, Alan M. *Supreme Injustice: How the High Court Hijacked Election 2000.* New York: Oxford University Press, 2001.

Gormley, Beatrice. *President George W. Bush: Our Forty-Third President.* New York: Aladdin Paperbacks, 2001.

Marsh, Carole, and Kathy Zimmer. *George W. Bush: America's Newest President and His White House Family.* The Here & Now series. Peachtree City, GA: Gallopade International, 2001.

Minutaglio, Bill. *First Son: George W. Bush and the Bush Family Dynasty.* New York: Random House, 1999.

Posner, Richard A. *Breaking the Deadlock: The 2000 Election, the Constitution, and the Courts.* Princeton, NJ: Princeton University Press, 2001.

Russell, Jon, ed. *The Complete Book of Inaugural Addresses of the Presidents of the United States: From George Washington to George W. Bush 1789 to 2001.* Seattle: iUniverse Online Books, 2001.

The White House
http://www.whitehouse.gov/president/gwbbio.html. This official White House biography of President George W. Bush offers a brief description of his life, career, and politics.

Woolf, Alex. *Osama bin Laden.* Minneapolis: Twenty-First Century Books, 2004.

INDEX

ABOUT THE AUTHOR

Herón Márquez, born in Mexico, moved to California at the age of six. After a short career playing semiprofessional baseball, he took up writing. He has worked as a journalist for such papers as the *Albuquerque Journal, New York Daily News, Los Angeles Times, Santa Barbara News Press,* and the *Minneapolis Star Tribune.* Márquez lives in Saint Paul, Minnesota, with his wife Traecy.

---- ✧ ----

PHOTO ACKNOWLEDGMENTS

The images in this book are used with the permission of: The White House, pp. 1, 2, 7, 11, 19, 25, 37, 47, 55, 63, 73, 89, 101; © Andy Nelson/*The Christian Science Monitor*/Getty Images, p. 6; © Brooks Kraft/CORBIS, pp. 8, 98 (right); George H. W. Bush Presidential Library, pp. 10, 13, 14, 17, 26, 29, 36, 49, 50; © Darren McCollester/Newsmakers/Getty Images, p. 21; Classmates.com Yearbook Archives, p. 22; © Rykoff Collection/CORBIS, p. 33; © Bettmann/CORBIS, pp. 34, 40, 42, 52, 60, 61; © Liaison Agency/Hulton Archive/Getty Images, p. 39; © Dave G. Houser/CORBIS, p. 56; © Dirck Halstead/Time Life Pictures/Getty Images, p. 58; Richard Michael Pruitt/The *Dallas Morning News,* p. 65; © Greg Smith/CORBIS, p. 66; AP/Wide World Photos, pp. 67, 82; © Tom Mihalek/AFP/Getty Images, p. 69; © Jana Birchum, p. 71; © Paul J. Richards/AFP/Getty Images, pp. 75, 88; © Reuters/CORBIS p. 76; © Shawn Thew/AFP/Getty Images, p. 79; © Chris Hondros/Newsmakers/Getty Images, p. 83; © Mark Wilson/Newsmakers/Getty Images, p. 86; © Jeff Haynes/AFP/Getty Images, p. 90; © Getty Images, p. 91; © Greg Martin/SuperStock, p. 92; © PPS Vienna/ZUMA Press, p. 95; © Ahmad Al-Rubaye/AFP/Getty Images, p. 97; © Justin Sullivan/Getty Images, p. 98 (left); © Andrew Parsons/AFP/Getty Images, p. 100; © Win McNamee/Getty Images, p. 103.

Cover: © Brooks Kraft/CORBIS.